South Africa
For Kids
People, Places and Cultures
Children Explore The World Books

Speedy Publishing LLC
40 E. Main St. #1156
Newark, DE 19711
www.speedypublishing.com

Let's learn some interesting facts about South Africa!

The official name
of South Africa
is the Republic
of South Africa.

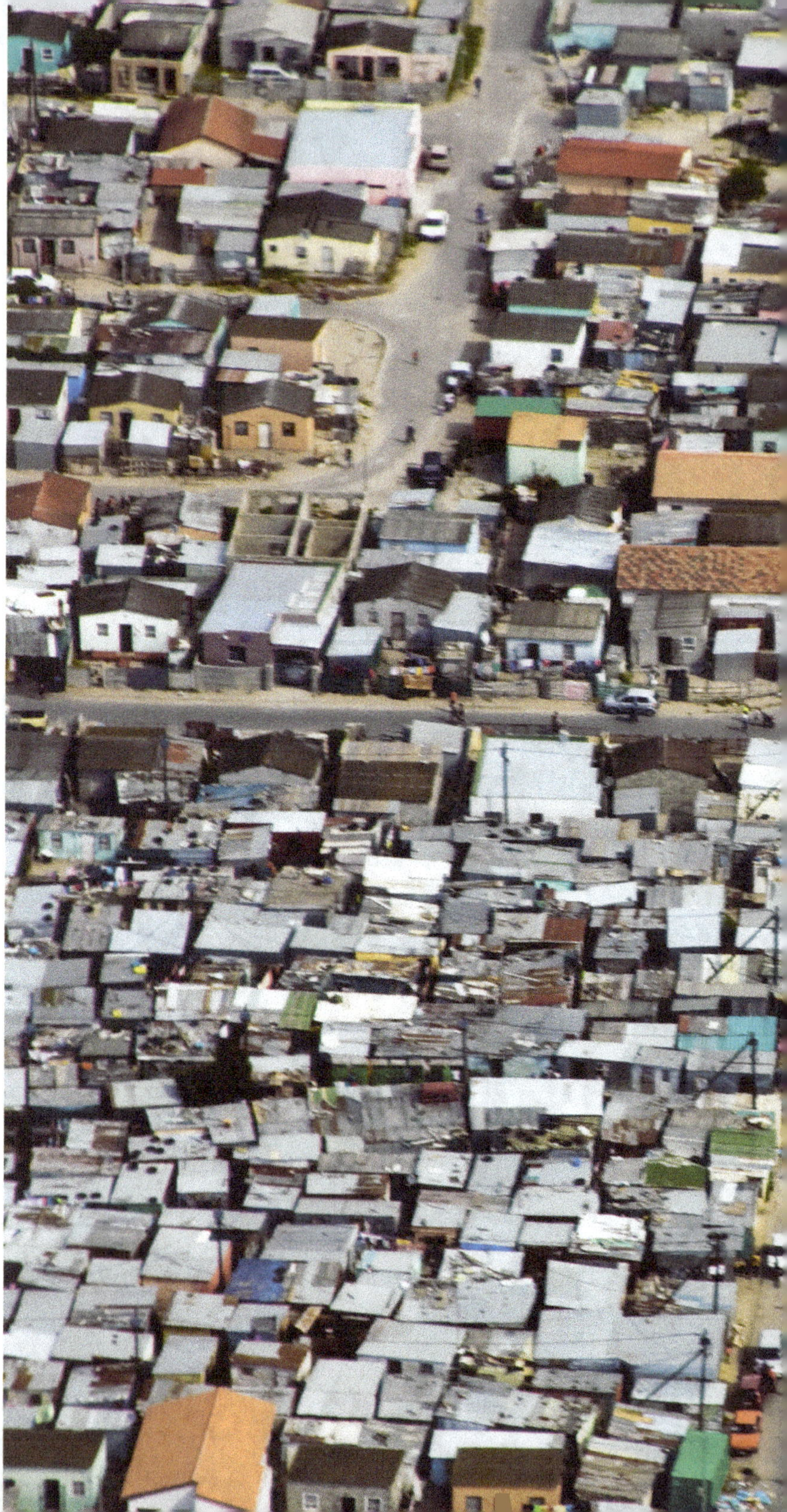

In 2011 the
population of
South Africa
was around
52 million.

South Africa has three capital cities, Cape Town, Bloemfontein and Pretoria.

South Africa has 11 official languages, including Zulu, Afrikaans, Xhosa and English.

South Africa has the largest economy of any African country.

Nelson Mandela was elected president in 1994 after South Africa's first universal elections.

South Africa's coastline stretches over 2500 kilometres (1553 miles) in length.

South Africa
is home to a
wide variety of
animals including
giraffes,
hippopotamus,
leopards
and lions.

**South Africa
has high
unemployment.**

The first
human heart
transplant was
performed
in a Cape
Town hospital
in 1967.

Cave paintings
have been found
in South Africa
that date to around
75000 years ago.

South Africa's
drinking water
is rated 3rd best
in the world for
being "safe and
ready to drink".

South Africa is
the only country
in the entire
world that has
voluntarily
abandoned its
nuclear weapons
programme.

South Africa is home to the oldest meteor scar in the world – the Vredefort Dome in a town called Parys. The site is a UNESCO World Heritage Site.

South Africa is home to the highest commercial bungi jump in the world at 710 feet.

The South
African
Rovos Rail is
considered
the most
luxurious train
in the world.

The oldest remains of modern humans were found in South Africa and are well over 160,000 years old.

South Africa

has a lot to offer and you should visit the country soon and explore!

Visit

BABY PROFESSOR
EDUCATION KIDS

www.BabyProfessorBooks.com
to download Free Baby Professor eBooks
and view our catalog of new and exciting
Children's Books